Probability

Unit guide

The School Mathematics Project

The right of the
University of Cambridge
to print and sell
all manner of books
was granted by
Henry VIII in 1534.
The University has printed
and published continuously
since 1584.

Cambridge University Press

Cambridge   New York   Port Chester   Melbourne   Sydney

Main authors	Chris Belsom
	Stan Dolan
	Leslie Glickman
	Ron Haydock
Project director	Stan Dolan

The authors would like to give special thanks to Ann White for her help in preparing this book for publication.

Published by the Press Syndicate of the University of Cambridge
The Pitt Building, Trumpington Street, Cambridge CB2 1RP
40 West 20th Street, New York, NY 10011-4211, USA
10 Stamford Road, Oakleigh, Melbourne 3166, Australia

First published 1991

Produced by 16-19 Mathematics, Southampton

Printed in Great Britain by Scotprint Ltd., Musselburgh.

ISBN 0 521 42656 1

Contents

Introduction to the unit
(for the teacher)

Although the subject matter of *Probability* is largely traditional it is hoped that students will find this book more appealing and more accessible than other introductory texts. As in all *16-19 Mathematics* units they will be actively involved and to a large degree the examples and exercises used relate to real life.

It is recognised that many students working through this unit may be doing so without the benefit of substantial contact time with a teacher. The unit has therefore been written to facilitate 'supported self-study'. It is assumed that even a minimal allocation of teacher time will allow contact at the start and end of each chapter and so

*   solutions to all thinking points and exercises are in the students' text;

*   a substantial discussion point in one of the opening sections enables the teacher to introduce each chapter;

*   a special tutorial sheet can be used to focus discussion at a final tutorial on the work of the chapter.

A few concepts from the *16-19 Mathematics* text *Living with uncertainty* are met again in this unit. Students who have read the earlier text should find their understanding enriched by revising these ideas in new contexts. Set language and notation, including the use of Venn diagrams, are used in defining probabilities where the members of a sample space are equally likely. Matrix multiplication is used in the treatment of Markov chains. Supplementary tasksheets are provided for students with no previous knowledge of these topics.

Chapter 1

The nature of probability is briefly explored, observed probabilities being contrasted with probabilities determined by symmetry. Set notation is used in introducing the concepts of mutually exclusive and independent events, leading to the formulation of the addition and multiplication laws. Finally, an example involving selection and arrangement motivates the treatment of permutations and combinations.

Chapter 2

Tree diagrams are used in analysing sequences of Bernoulli trials and also in introducing conditional probabilities. Bernoulli sequences lead naturally to a study of the binomial distribution and a tasksheet on a continuous probability distribution is also included. The concept of conditional probability leads to Bayes' theorem and its applications.

Chapter 3

Problems involving selection and arrangement and associated probabilities are handled using occupancy models. The models are used in solving two classical puzzles - the 'birthday' and 'derangement' problems. The process of 'reasoning by renewal' is introduced and used in forming recurrence relations. Problems met at this stage include 'gambler's ruin', which is seen to involve a random walk in one dimension. Finally, a method for solving linear recurrence relations is introduced.

An extensive tutorial tasksheet checks the important ideas covered in this chapter.

Chapter 4

Transition diagrams and matrices are used in the study of Markov chains. The gambler's ruin problem is seen to involve a Markov chain. Bernoulli and Markov sequences are compared and contrasted by considering lengths of runs of the possible outcomes. Finally, a method of finding the steady state vector for a convergent Markov sequence is explained.

Chapter 5

Simulation is introduced as a method of modelling sequences of events which are determined probabilistically. The use of a computer or calculator is encouraged and algorithms to generate pseudo-random numbers are described. Continuous variables are simulated using a Monte Carlo method.

To give students time to tackle a simulation project, the text and tasksheets for this chapter contain only a few questions.

Tasksheets

1 First ideas

1.1 Introduction

> **(a)** List the ways in which the competition could have finished.
>
> **(b)** How should the stake be divided?
>
> **(c)** In a similar incomplete competition, how should the stake be divided when
>
>   (i) *A* needs one more win and *B* needs three;
>   (ii) *A* needs two more wins and *B* needs three?

(a) The possible sequences for winners of the remaining games are:

$$A, \ BA, \ BB.$$

(b) A first reaction might be to note that two out of three ways favour *A*, so that perhaps the stake should be divided in the ratio 2 : 1. A more searching analysis reveals that the three ways *A, BA, BB* are not **equally likely.**

One way of illustrating the possibilities is to use a **tree diagram.**

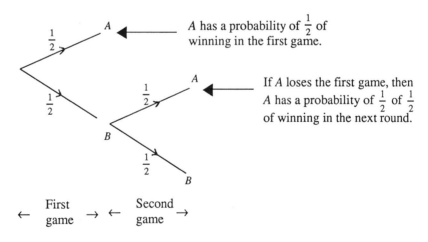

A has a probability of $\frac{1}{2}$ of winning in the first game.

If A loses the first game, then A has a probability of $\frac{1}{2}$ of $\frac{1}{2}$ of winning in the next round.

$\leftarrow$ First game $\rightarrow$ $\leftarrow$ Second game $\rightarrow$

The total probability is $\frac{1}{2} + \left(\frac{1}{2} \times \frac{1}{2}\right) = \frac{3}{4}$

The stake should be divided in the ratio 3 : 1.

(c) In the solution below, a tree diagram is used in the first case and a set of equally likely outcomes in the second. Both problems may, of course, be solved by either method and you are encouraged to demonstrate the alternative approach to each.

(i)

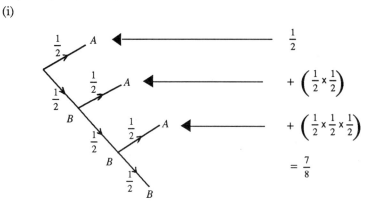

The stake should be divided in the ratio 7 : 1.

(ii) Suppose that a further 4 games had been played. The set of all possible outcomes is:

{ *AAAA* , *AAAB*, *AABA*, *ABAA*, *BAAA*, *AABB*, *ABAB*, *ABBA*, *BAAB*, *BABA*, *BBAA*, ABBB, BABB, BBAB, BBBA, BBBB }

These 16 possibilities are all equally likely. The members underlined form the subset favourable to A. Out of 16 equally likely outcomes, 11 favour A, so the stake should be divided in the ratio 11 : 5.

The algebra of sets

1.   (a) $A \cap B = \{ 2, 4 \} \Rightarrow (A \cap B)' = \{ 1, 3, 5, 6, 7, 8, 9, 10 \}$.

              $A' = \{ 1, 3, 5, 7, 9 \}$, $B' = \{ 5, 6, 7, 8, 9, 10 \}$

              $\Rightarrow A' \cup B' = \{ 1, 3, 5, 6, 7, 8, 9, 10 \}$.

   (b)

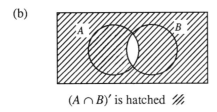 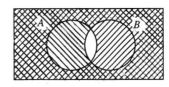

         $(A \cap B)'$ is hatched ///

                                  A' is hatched ///
                                  B' is hatched \\\
                                  Everything hatched makes up $A' \cup B'$

2.   (a) $P(B) = \dfrac{4}{10}$

   (b) $P(B') = \dfrac{6}{10}$

        $P(B) + P(B') = 1$

   (c) $P(A \cup B) + P(A \cap B) = \dfrac{7}{10} + \dfrac{2}{10} = \dfrac{9}{10}$

                 $P(A) + P(B) = \dfrac{5}{10} + \dfrac{4}{10}$

        $P(A \cup B) + P(A \cap B) = P(A) + P(B)$

Hands of cards

1.   (a)   52,   (b)   51,   (c)   52 x 51 ordered pairs

      (d)   52 x 51 x 50 x 49 ordered sets of four cards can be dealt.

2.   (a)   Each hand of two cards gives two possible ordered pairs. For example (2 of diamonds, ace of clubs) and (ace of clubs, 2 of diamonds) form the same hand.

         So there are $\frac{52 \times 51}{2}$ possible hands of two cards.

      (b)   Each hand of three cards gives 3 x 2 x 1 = 6 distinct ordered triples.

         There are $\frac{52 \times 51 \times 50}{6}$ possible hands of 3 cards.

      (c)   Similarly there are $\frac{52 \times 51 \times 50 \times 49}{4 \times 3 \times 2 \times 1}$ hands of 4 cards,

         [A convenient notation for 4 x 3 x 2 x 1 is 4! , read as '4 factorial'].

3.   (a) $H_5 = \frac{52 \times 51 \times 50 \times 49 \times 48}{5 \times 4 \times 3 \times 2 \times 1}$

      (b) $H_5 = \frac{48}{5} \times \frac{52 \times 51 \times 50 \times 49}{4 \times 3 \times 2 \times 1} = \frac{48}{5} \times H_4$

      (c) $H_6 = \frac{47}{6} \times H_5$

         $H_{n+1} = \frac{52-n}{n+1} \times H_n$.

      (d)   The factors $\frac{51}{2}$, $\frac{50}{3}$ $\cdots$ can be used successively to find H_2 , H_3 ,... This is a rapid procedure if you use a calculator or short program. Later values in the table are given to three significant figures.

n	1	2	3	4	5	6	7
H_n	52	1326	22100	2.71×10^5	2.60×10^6	2.04×10^7	1.34×10^8

n	8	9	10	11	12	13
H_n	7.53×10^8	3.68×10^9	1.58×10^{10}	6.04×10^{10}	2.06×10^{11}	6.35×10^{11}

      (e)   The probability of being dealt any given hand is 1 in 6.35×10^{11}.

(continued)

4. (a) By extension of the answers in question 1, the number of ordered sets of r cards is the product of r factors, starting from 52 and decreasing by 1 each time, i.e.

$$52 \times 51 \times \ldots \times (52 - r + 1) = \frac{52 \times 51 \times \ldots \times (52 - r + 1) \times (52 - r) \times \ldots \times 2 \times 1}{(52 - r) \times \ldots \times 2 \times 1}$$

$$= \frac{52\,!}{(52 - r)\,!}$$

(b) Each hand of r cards gives $r\,!$ ordered sets of r cards.

$$H_r = \frac{52\,!}{(52 - r)\,!} \div r\,! = \frac{52\,!}{(52 - r)\,!\, r\,!}$$

(c) From a set of n cards, the number of ordered sets of r cards is $\dfrac{n\,!}{(n - r)\,!}$

The number of hands of r cards is $\dfrac{n\,!}{(n - r)\,!\, r\,!}$.

Tutorial sheet

1. In this commentary, only the theoretical probabilities are calculated. Observed probabilities for small numbers of samples will often be poor approximations to these. For large numbers the approximations should be much better.

    (a) $P(\{R, B, Y\}) = \dfrac{10 \times 6 \times 4}{\binom{20}{3}} = \dfrac{4}{19} \approx 0.21$

    (b) $P(R \text{ then } B \text{ then } Y) = \dfrac{10}{20} \times \dfrac{6}{19} \times \dfrac{4}{18} = \dfrac{2}{57} \approx 0.035$

    Note that $0.035 \times 3! = 0.21$. The expressions for the two probabilities in (a) and (b) may be manipulated to demonstrate this relationship.

2. (a) $P(\{R, R, B, Y\}) = \dfrac{\binom{10}{2} \times 6 \times 4}{\binom{20}{4}} = \dfrac{72}{323} \approx 0.22$

    (b) $P(R \text{ then } B \text{ then } R \text{ then } Y) = \dfrac{10}{20} \times \dfrac{6}{19} \times \dfrac{9}{18} \times \dfrac{4}{17} = \dfrac{6}{323} \approx 0.019.$

    The first probability is $\dfrac{4!}{2!}$ times the second, since each set of 2 reds, 1 blue and 1 yellow may be arranged in $\dfrac{4!}{2!}$ ways.

3. (a) Three of one suit, 4 possibilities.
    Two of one suit, one of another, $4 \times 3 = 12$ possibilities.
    All of different suits, $4 \times 3 \times 2 = 24$ possibilities. ✗ (*why should order matter?*)

    $4 + 12 + \cancel{24} = \cancel{40}\ 20$ *So* $\binom{4}{3} = 4$

    (b) The most 'balanced' hand is most likely; in a hand of four, one of each suit; in a hand of five, two of one suit, one of each of the others; in a hand of six, two of two suits, one of each of the two others.   *4 cards ⟹ 31 distinct hands*

4. The most balanced hand is most likely; three cards in each of three suits and four in the remaining suit.

2 n-stage experiments

2.3 The binomial distribution

> **(a)** Write out the complete expansion of $(p + q)^4$.
>
> **(b)** Verify that the probabilities P(2 S's, 2 N's), P(1 S, 3 N's) are given by the next two terms in this expansion

(a) $$(p+q)^4 = \binom{4}{0}p^4 + \binom{4}{1}p^3q + \binom{4}{2}p^2q^2 + \binom{4}{3}pq^3 + \binom{4}{4}q^4$$

$$= p^4 + 4p^3q + 6p^2q^2 + 4pq^3 + q^4$$

(b) $$\text{P(2 S's, 2 N's)} = 6 \times \left(\frac{1}{6}\right)^2 \left(\frac{5}{6}\right)^2 = 6p^2q^2$$

$$\text{P(1 S, 3 N's)} = 4 \times \left(\frac{1}{6}\right) \left(\frac{5}{6}\right)^3 = 4pq^3$$

Each term in the expansion of $(p + q)^4$ is obtained by choosing either p or q from each of the four bracketed expressions:

$$(p + q)^4 = (p + q)\,(p + q)\,(p + q)\,(p + q)$$

$$= pppp \quad + \quad pppq + ppqp + pqpp + qppp + \ldots$$

Considering just the p^3q terms, it can be seen that they correspond precisely to the four 'routes',

$$\text{SSSN, SSNS, SNSS, NSSS.}$$

There is a similar correspondence between the other terms of $(p + q)^4$ and the other combinations of sixes and not-sixes.

1. $p^2 + 2pq + q^2 = (p + q)^2 = 1$, since $p + q = 1$.

2. (a) Second line:

$$P(\text{father } SS, \text{ mother } SN) = p^2 \times 2pq = 2p^3q$$
$$P(\text{mother } SS, \text{ father } SN) = p^2 \times 2pq = 2p^3q$$
$$\Rightarrow P(\text{one } SS, \text{ other } SN) = 4p^3q$$

One parent always provides an S allele. The other has equal chances of providing an S or an N allele.

Similar explanations can be given for the first and fourth lines.

(b)

		Assuming the event		
Event	P(Event)	P(SS)	P(SN)	P(NN)
SS, SS	p^4	1	0	0
SS, SN	$4p^3q$	$\frac{1}{2}$	$\frac{1}{2}$	0
SS, NN	$2p^2q^2$	0	1	0
SN, SN	$4p^2q^2$	$\frac{1}{4}$	$\frac{1}{2}$	$\frac{1}{4}$
SN, NN	$4pq^3$	0	$\frac{1}{2}$	$\frac{1}{2}$
NN, NN	q^4	0	0	1

(c) From the table, for the following generation,

$$P(SS) = p^4 + \frac{1}{2}(4p^3q) + \frac{1}{4}(4p^2q^2)$$
$$= p^4 + 2p^3q + p^2q^2$$
$$= p^2(p^2 + 2pq + q^2) = p^2(p + q)^2 = p^2$$

Similarly, $P(SN) = 2pq$ and $P(NN) = q^2$.

3. From question 2 it may be concluded that in the case when the probability distribution is p^2, $2pq$, q^2, with random pairing the distribution remains stable. To show that the distribution always tends to the stable form might be a suitable topic for a project.

4. The SS and NS alleles together have probability $p^2 + 2pq$. Hence $p^2 + 2pq = 0.2$.

Then $p^2 + 2p(1 - p) = 0.2 \Rightarrow p^2 - 2p + 0.2 = 0$
$p = 1 - \sqrt{0.8} \approx 0.011$ (ignoring the root $p > 1$)

The percentage of SS genotypes would be 1.1%.

A continuous probability model

1.   The area of triangle ABC is 1 since all the rods have a length in the range 24.8 - 25.2 cm.

2.   (a)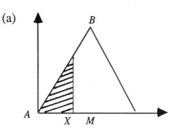

Since the shaded triangle and triangle ABM are similar,

$$\frac{\text{area of shaded } \Delta}{\text{area of } \Delta ABM} = \left(\frac{AX}{AM}\right)^2 = \left(\frac{x-24.8}{25.0-24.8}\right)^2$$

The area of triangle ABM is $\frac{1}{2}$. So the shaded area is $\frac{1}{2}\left(\frac{x-24.8}{25.0-24.8}\right)^2$.

(b)   P(length between 24.8 and x) $= \frac{1}{2}\left(\frac{x-24.8}{0.2}\right)^2 = \frac{25}{2}(x-24.8)^2$

P(length between 24.8 and 25.0) $= \frac{1}{2}$

P(length between 24.8 and 24.9) $= \frac{25}{2}(24.9-24.8)^2 = \frac{1}{8}$

P(length between 24.9 and 25.0) $= \frac{1}{2} - \frac{1}{8} = \frac{3}{8}$

P(length between 24.9 and 25.1) $= 2 \times \frac{3}{8} = \frac{3}{4}$

3.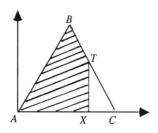

P(length between 24.8 and x) = 1 − area of triangle TXC. The area of triangle TXC may be found using similar triangles and is

$$\frac{1}{2}\left(\frac{25.2-x}{25.2-25.0}\right)^2 = \frac{25}{2}(25.2-x)^2$$

The required probability is $1 - \frac{25}{2}(25.2-x)^2$.

(continued)

17

4.

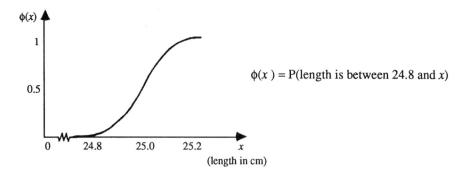

$\phi(x) = P(\text{length is between 24.8 and } x)$

You can use the formula in question 2 to build up a table of values for $\phi(x)$

x	24.8	24.85	24.90	24.95	25.0
$\phi(x)$	0	0.031	0.125	0.281	0.500

Values for $x > 25.0$ may be found by symmetry.

5. From the graph (or by calculation), $\phi^{-1}(0.025) = 24.845$.

Hence $t = 25.000 - 24.845 = 0.155$.

Colour blindness

1.   Of the 1000 adults you should expect 1000 x 0.03 to be colour blind, i.e. 30 individuals.

   (a)   500 x 0.05 = 25
   (b)   500 – 25   = 475
   (c)   30 – 25   =   5
   (d)   500 – 5   = 495

2. $P(C \mid M) = 0.05$.

3. $P(C' \mid F)$ is the probability of being colour blind given that the subject is female.
   It is $\frac{495}{500} = 0.99$.

4.

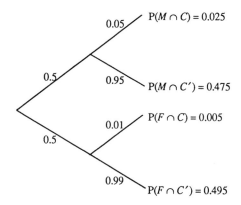

   0.05 → $P(M \cap C) = 0.025$

   0.5

   0.95 → $P(M \cap C') = 0.475$

   0.01 → $P(F \cap C) = 0.005$

   0.5

   0.99 → $P(F \cap C') = 0.495$

5. $\dfrac{P(M \cap C)}{P(M)} = \dfrac{0.025}{0.5} = 0.05 = P(C \mid M)$

6.   (a) $P(C' \mid M) = \dfrac{P(M \cap C')}{P(M)}$ (b) $P(C \mid F) = \dfrac{P(F \cap C)}{P(F)}$

   (c) $P(C' \mid F) = \dfrac{P(F \cap C')}{P(F)}$

7. $P(C) = P(M \cap C) + P(F \cap C)$

          $= P(M)\,P(C \mid M) + P(F)\,P(C \mid F)$

1.

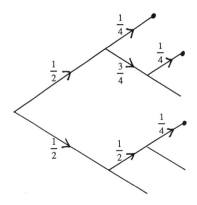

$$\frac{1}{2} \times \frac{1}{4} + \frac{1}{2} \times \frac{3}{4} \times \frac{1}{4} + \frac{1}{2} \times \frac{1}{2} \times \frac{1}{4} = \frac{9}{32}$$

⑦

2. (a)

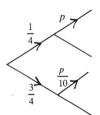

(b) $P(F \mid S) = \dfrac{P(F \cap S)}{P(S)} = \dfrac{\frac{3}{4} \times \frac{p}{10}}{\frac{1}{4}p + \frac{3}{40}p} = \dfrac{3}{13}$.

This assumes that the proportion of the sexes and the gender related promotion prospects have remained constant.

 ⑧

(continued)

3.   With the natural notation:

$P(S) = 0.5,$ $P(W \mid S) = 0.2$
$P(L) = 0.3,$ $P(W \mid L) = 0.3$
$P(H) = 0.2,$ $P(W \mid H) = 0.9$

$P(W) = 0.5 \times 0.2 + 0.3 \times 0.3 + 0.2 \times 0.9$
$= 0.37$

$P(S \mid W) = \dfrac{P(S \cap W)}{P(W)} = \dfrac{0.1}{0.37} \approx 0.27$

$P(L \mid W) = \dfrac{0.09}{0.37} \approx 0.24$

$P(H \mid W) = \dfrac{0.18}{0.37} \approx 0.49$

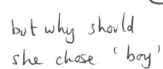 *Mention Accuracy*

⑧

4.   (a)   A priori, there are four equally likely events   */ but why should she chose 'boy'*

$BB, BG, GB, GG.$

Knowing that GG has not occurred leaves three equally likely possibilities. So $P(BB) = \dfrac{1}{3}$.

⑦

      (b)   Knowing that the youngest is a boy means that there are only two equally likely possibilities, BB and BG. So $P(BB) = \dfrac{1}{2}$.

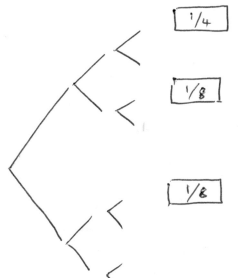

she says 'at least one of my children is a boy'

$1/4$

$1/8$

$1/8$

$p(2 \text{ boys} \mid \text{she } \underline{\text{says}} \text{ "...")}$

$= \dfrac{1/4}{1/4 + \frac{1}{8} + \frac{1}{8}} = \dfrac{1}{2}$

21

3 Occupancy and random walks

3.1 Counting problems

> From a group of four students, Armand, Brian, Cheryl and Diane, you are to choose a committee.
>
> In how many ways can you do this if:
>
> (a)   a committee of two is to be chosen, both members having equal status;
>
> (b)   a chairperson and a treasurer are to be chosen, the jobs being given to different students;
>
> (c)   a chairperson and a treasurer are to be chosen, and the same student can assume both tasks?

(a)   Allocate **unlabelled** tokens to the boxes so that no box contains more than one token.

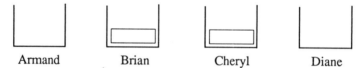

The number of committees is simply the number of choices of 2 boxes from 4 i.e. $\binom{4}{2} = 6$.

(b)   Label the two tokens [chair] [treasurer]

The number of ordered choices of pairs of boxes is $_4P_2 = 12$. This is the number of possible committees.

(c)   An allocation such as the following is now possible:

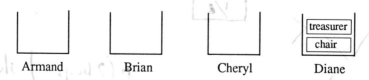

Allocate the first task to any of the students; this can be done in 4 ways. Allocate the second task to any of the students; again this can be done in 4 possible ways. The basic multiplication rule then says that there are 4 x 4 = 16 possible committees.

why not allocate posts and fill them

Birthdays and birthmates

1.   (a)   Model 3 applies. There are $5^3 = 125$ possible allocations.

    (b)   Model 2 applies. There are $_5P_3 = 60$ allocations.

    (c)   From (a) and (b) there are $125 - 60 = 65$ allocations in which at least two tickets appear in the same box. The required probability is $\frac{65}{125} = 0.52$.

2.   (a)   As in question 1, there are 365^r possible allocations of which $_{365}P_r$ are rejected as ones in which the students all have different birthdays.

$$P(\text{at least two students have the same birthday}) = \frac{365^r - _{365}P_r}{365^r}$$

3. $Q_j = \dfrac{365 \times 364 \times \ldots \times (365 - j)}{365^{j-1}} \times \dfrac{365 - j + 1}{365}$

$\qquad = Q_{j-1} \times \dfrac{365 - j + 1}{365}$

The required probability is $1 - Q_r$.

The sequence (Q_n) starts with $Q_1 = 1$. Then

$Q_2 = 1 \times \dfrac{364}{365} = \dfrac{364}{365}, \quad Q_3 = \dfrac{364}{365} \times \dfrac{363}{365}, \ldots$

You will find that $Q_{23} = 0.4927$ is the first member of the sequence less than 0.5. The required number is $r = 23$.

4.   Of the 5^3 possible allocations, those in which box number 1 contains no token are cases when the tickets are all in the four remaining boxes, and there are 4^3 of these. Box number 1 will have at least one ticket in $(5^3 - 4^3)$ cases.

The required probability is $\dfrac{5^3 - 4^3}{5^3} = 0.488$

5.   Using the same reasoning,

$$P(\text{box number 1 contains at least one ticket}) = \frac{365^r - 364^r}{365^r}$$

$$= 1 - \left(\frac{364}{365}\right)^r$$

(continued)

6.   (a)   Your birthday may be regarded as box number 1, so the required probability is

$$1 - \left(\frac{364}{365}\right)^{r-1}$$

7. $Q_j = \left(\frac{364}{365}\right)^j = \left(\frac{364}{365}\right)^{j-1} \times \frac{364}{365} = Q_{j-1} \times \frac{364}{365}$

The required value of r is 253.

8.   In the birthday problem you are interested in allocations where **any** box contains two or more tickets; whereas in the birthmate problem a **particular** box must be occupied. As a result, in the birthday problem the probability reaches 1 when $r = 365$; in the birthmate problem it never reaches 1.

Derangement probabilities

1.

n	1	2	3	4
d_n	0	1	2	9
$n!$	1	2	6	24
p_n	0	0.500	0.333	0.375

note – why?

The nine derangements of $ABCD$ are

BADC, BCDA, BDAC,
CDAB, CADB, CDBA,
DCBA, DABC, DCAB.

what is the limit?

$\frac{1}{e}$!

2. (a) If A and B swap hats then any derangement of CDE results in a derangement of the whole set. The same argument applies to the other three splits: AC/BDE, AD/BCE and AE/BCD.

(b) If A has E's hat but E does not have A's then any derangement of $EBCD$ results in a derangement of the whole set. It may be helpful to consider allocation to boxes.

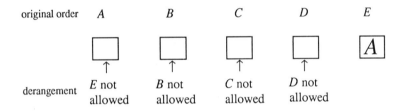

The same argument applies if A has the hat of B, C or D. So there are $4 \times d_4$ derangements of this type.

3. $d_5 = 4d_3 + 4d_4 = (4 \times 2) + (4 \times 9) = 44$.

4. $d_6 = 5d_4 + 5d_5 = 265$

$d_7 = 6d_5 + 6d_6 = 1854$

5. (a) In general it is helpful to think of derangments of the numbers 1, 2, 3, ..., n rather than hats.

If 1 is interchanged with any other number then a derangement of the remaining $(n-2)$ numbers results in a derangement of the whole set. Since $(n-1)$ such interchanges are possible there are $(n-1)\,d_{n-2}$ derangements of this type.

If 1 has taken the rth position but r does not take the 1st position then any derangement of the $(n-1)$ numbers

$$r, 2, 3, \ldots, (r-1), (r+1), \ldots, n$$

results in a derangement of the whole set. Since r may be chosen in $(n-1)$ ways there are $(n-1)\,d_{n-1}$ derangements of this type.

(continued)

25

In any derangement, 1 either interchanges with another number or takes the place of another number without interchange; so the two types of derangements considered above include all possible cases. Hence

$$d_n = (n-1)\, d_{n-2} + (n-1)\, d_{n-1}.$$

(b)
$$P_n - P_{n-1} = \frac{d_n}{n!} - \frac{d_{n-1}}{(n-1)!}$$

$$= \frac{(n-1)\, d_{n-1} + (n-1)\, d_{n-2}}{n!} - \frac{d_{n-1}}{(n-1)!} \qquad \text{[using the recurrence relation]}$$

$$= \frac{-d_{n-1} + (n-1)\, d_{n-2}}{n!}$$

$$= -\frac{1}{n}\left[\frac{d_{n-1}}{(n-1)!} - \frac{d_{n-2}}{(n-2)!}\right]$$

$$= -\frac{1}{n}\,(P_{n-1} - P_{n-2})$$

(c)
$$P_2 - P_1 = \tfrac{1}{2}, \quad \text{so } P_3 - P_2 = -\tfrac{1}{3} \times \tfrac{1}{2}$$

$$P_4 - P_3 = \tfrac{1}{4} \times \tfrac{1}{3} \times \tfrac{1}{2}$$

$$P_5 - P_4 = -\tfrac{1}{5} \times \tfrac{1}{4} \times \tfrac{1}{3} \times \tfrac{1}{2}$$

$$\dots$$

$$P_n - P_{n-1} = (-1)^n\, \frac{1}{n!}$$

6. $$P_n = P_1 + (P_2 - P_1) + \dots + (P_n - P_{n-1})$$

$$= 0 + \frac{1}{2!} - \frac{1}{3!} + \dots + (-1)^n\, \frac{1}{n!}$$

The term 0 can be replaced by $\frac{1}{0!} - \frac{1}{1!}$ to give the required result.

7.   The expansion is the first $(n+1)$ terms of the series expansion of e^{-1}.

If the series is taken as far as the term $\frac{1}{7!}$ its sum of 0.3679 already agrees with e^{-1} to four decimal places, so the probability of a derangement of n hats is very nearly e^{-1} for $n > 6$.

Gambler's ruin

1.   The given diagram is equivalent to

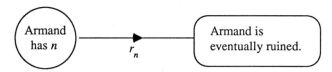

So $r_n = pr_{n+1} + qr_{n-1}$.

2.   If Armand has 0 then he is already ruined, so $r_0 = 1$. If Armand has a then Cheryl is ruined and Armand cannot be ruined, so $r_a = 0$.

3.   If $p = q = \frac{1}{2}$ and $r_n = \frac{a-n}{a}$ then

$$pr_{n+1} + qr_{n-1} = \frac{1}{2} \times \frac{a-n-1}{a} + \frac{1}{2} \times \frac{a-n+1}{a}$$

$$= \frac{1}{2a}(a-n-1+a-n+1)$$

$$= \frac{a-n}{a} = r_n$$

Also $r_0 = \frac{a-0}{a} = 1$ and $r_a = \frac{a-a}{a} = 0$.

If $p = q = \frac{1}{2}$ then when Armand has n the ratio of his chance of winning to Cheryl's is the same as the ratio of their capitals, i.e. $\frac{n}{a-n}$.

So the probability of his eventual ruin is $\dfrac{a-n}{a-n+n} = \dfrac{a-n}{a}$

4.   Let $\frac{q}{p} = x$. Then, if $r_n = \dfrac{x^a - x^n}{x^a - 1}$,

$$pr_{n+1} + qr_{n-1} = \frac{p\left(x^a - x^{n+1}\right) + q\left(x^a - x^{n-1}\right)}{x^a - 1}$$

$$= \frac{(p+q)x^a - x^n\left(px + \frac{q}{x}\right)}{x^a - 1}$$

$$= \frac{x^a - x^n}{x^a - 1} \quad \text{[using } x = \frac{q}{p} \text{ and } p + q = 1\text{]}$$

$$= r_n, \text{ as required.}$$

1. Associate a box with each of the six faces of the die. Each throw will correspond to a token. Any box may contain more than one token since the throws can result in a particular face appearing more than once. Using model 3 with $n = 6$ and $r = 6$, the total number of possible allocations is 6^6.

    The number of possibilities which give rise to all six faces occurring is found using model 2 with $n = 6$ and $r = 6$. The number of possibilities is $_6P_6 = 6!$ and the probability of the event is $\dfrac{6!}{6^6} = \dfrac{5}{324}$.

2. Consider the 6 chairs as boxes and the 4 patients as distinguishable tokens. Occupancy model 2 applies with $n = 6$ and $r = 4$ and the number of possible distributions is $_6P_4 = 360$.

    There are 3 configurations such that all occupied chairs are adjacent:

    Each of these corresponds to $_4P_4 = 24$ distributions. Assuming that patients choose chairs at random, the probability of this event is therefore $\dfrac{3 \times 24}{360} = \dfrac{1}{5}$.

3. (a) represents 'double-1' and so on.

    (b) There are $\binom{7}{2} = 21$ allocations in which each box contains at most one token. There are another 7 allocations corresponding to 'doubles'.

    (c) A model of type 1 is

    The configuration shown represents 'double-1'.

4. The probability of a derangement of 13 objects is

    $$\frac{1}{2!} - \frac{1}{3!} + \ldots - \frac{1}{13!} \approx e^{-1} \approx 0.3679$$

    P(not derangement) $\approx 1 - 0.3679 = 0.6321$

    $1 - \dfrac{229079390932}{13!}$

    This is a good example of the sort of gambling game where the punters think they stand an even chance, the banker knows they do not!

(continued)

Ignore differences in black/white

5.   (a)   Note that p is the probability of winning, having just won a game. Let 'success' mean 'Clare is first to win two successive games'.

Success may occur in the second game, or in a later game as shown:

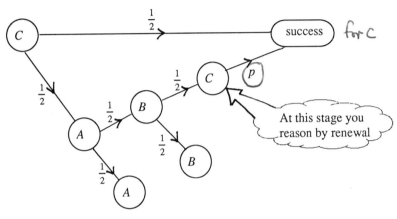

for C

At this stage you reason by renewal

Then $p = \frac{1}{2} + \frac{1}{8}p$.

(b)   In the next diagram 'success' means 'Ahmed is first to win two successive games'. Note that when he has just won a game, P(success) = p and that when he has just lost a game, P(success) = $\frac{1}{4}p$, as in the diagram above.

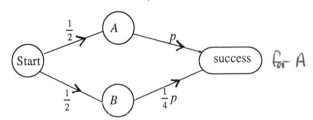

for A

P(Ahmed succeeds) = $\frac{1}{2}p + \frac{1}{8}p$

From the equation in (a), $p = \frac{4}{7}$.

So P(Ahmed succeeds) = $\frac{5}{8} \times \frac{4}{7} = \frac{5}{14}$.

(6)

(continued)

29

6.   (a)   P(face 1 not underneath after n moves) $= 1 - p_n$.
Given that face 1 is not underneath,
P(next move brings face 1 underneath) $= \frac{1}{3}$.

Hence $p_{n+1} = \frac{1}{3}(1 - p_n)$

Initial Sol^n

Particular Sol^n

(b)   Then $p_n = \frac{1}{4} + A\left(-\frac{1}{3}\right)^n$ ← *expand*

= General Sol^n
value of A, B etc
and check

If $p_0 = 1$ then $A = \frac{3}{4}$ and

$$p_n = \frac{1}{4} + \frac{3}{4}\left(-\frac{1}{3}\right)^n$$

(c)   If n is large, $p_n \approx \frac{1}{4}$. In the long run each face is underneath with equal frequency.

    ⑥

OHP

7.   (a)   Since the counter remains on the board it must occupy one of the nine squares at any time, and

P(occupying a square) = P(corner square) + P(edge square) + P(middle square)

$$\Rightarrow 1 = 4c_n + 4e_n + m_n$$

must sum to 1

(b)   If at any stage the counter occupies an edge square then it has three equally likely moves. Two of these are to corner squares and this is the only way of reaching a corner square. So, for $n \geq 1$,

$$c_n = \frac{2}{3}e_{n-1} .$$ *2 × ½*

Similarly, $e_n = c_{n-1} + \frac{1}{4}m_{n-1}$ and $m_n = \frac{4}{3}e_{n-1}$.   *← 4 × ⅓*

OHP

(c)   From these relations,

$$e_n = \frac{2}{3}e_{n-2} + \frac{1}{4} \times \frac{4}{3}e_{n-2} ,\text{ for } n \geq 2.$$

So $e_n = e_{n-2}$, for $n \geq 2$.

Now $c_0 = e_0 = m_0 = \frac{1}{9}$ and $e_1 = c_0 + \frac{1}{4}m_0 = \frac{5}{36}$.

Therefore, $e_n = \begin{cases} \frac{1}{9} & \text{if } n \text{ is even} \\ \frac{5}{36} & \text{if } n \text{ is odd} \end{cases}$

    ⑥

or

$$e_n = \frac{9}{72} + \frac{1}{72}(-1)^{n+1}$$

4 Sequences of random events

4.2 Stochastic matrices

In a sequence of five–minute chess games with Alan, Beryl finds that if she has won the previous game she wins on three-quarters of occasions, whereas if she has lost previously there is only an even chance of her winning. The chance of a draw is negligible.

(a) Write down the stochastic matrix for Beryl's chess games.

(b) Given that Beryl wins the first game, show that the outcome probability vector for the second game is

$$\begin{pmatrix} P(W) \\ P(L) \end{pmatrix} = \begin{pmatrix} \frac{3}{4} \\ \frac{1}{4} \end{pmatrix}$$

(c) Use the tree diagram shown to find the outcome probability vector for the third game.

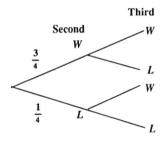

(d) By considering your answer to (c), describe how the elements of the stochastic matrix and the outcome probability vector for one game can be used to find the outcome probability vector for the next game.

(e) Hence find the outcome probability vector for the fourth game.

(a)

	B	A
B	$\frac{3}{4}$	$\frac{1}{2}$
A	$\frac{1}{4}$	$\frac{1}{2}$

(b) A win is followed by a win with probability $\frac{3}{4}$. Otherwise it is followed by a loss with probability $1 - \frac{3}{4} = \frac{1}{4}$.

31

(c)

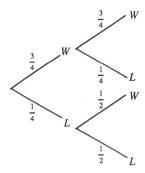

For the third game,

$$\begin{bmatrix} P(W) \\ P(L) \end{bmatrix} = \begin{bmatrix} \frac{3}{4} \times \frac{3}{4} + \frac{1}{4} \times \frac{1}{2} \\ \frac{1}{4} \times \frac{3}{4} + \frac{1}{4} \times \frac{1}{2} \end{bmatrix}$$

$$= \begin{bmatrix} \frac{11}{16} \\ \frac{5}{16} \end{bmatrix}$$

(d) Using the notation $\begin{bmatrix} p_n \\ q_n \end{bmatrix}$ for the nth outcome probability vector,

$$p_3 = \frac{3}{4} p_2 + \frac{1}{2} q_2$$
$$q_3 = \frac{1}{4} p_2 + \frac{1}{2} q_2$$

(e) Following the same pattern,

$$p_4 = \frac{3}{4} p_3 + \frac{1}{2} q_3 = \left(\frac{3}{4} \times \frac{11}{16} \right) + \left(\frac{1}{2} \times \frac{5}{16} \right) \approx 0.67$$

$$q_4 = \frac{1}{4} p_3 + \frac{1}{2} q_3 \approx 0.33$$

Matrix multiplication

1. $\mathbf{BA} = \begin{bmatrix} 1 & 4 \\ 6 & 1 \\ 5 & 9 \end{bmatrix} \begin{bmatrix} 4 & 2 & 8 \\ 3 & 3 & 7 \end{bmatrix} = \begin{bmatrix} 1 \times 4 + 4 \times 3 & 1 \times 2 + 4 \times 3 & 1 \times 8 + 4 \times 7 \\ 6 \times 4 + 1 \times 3 & 6 \times 2 + 1 \times 3 & 6 \times 8 + 1 \times 7 \\ 5 \times 4 + 9 \times 3 & 5 \times 2 + 9 \times 3 & 5 \times 8 + 9 \times 7 \end{bmatrix}$

$= \begin{bmatrix} 16 & 14 & 36 \\ 27 & 15 & 55 \\ 47 & 37 & 103 \end{bmatrix}$

2. $(\mathbf{AB})\mathbf{C} = \begin{bmatrix} 56 & 90 \\ 56 & 78 \end{bmatrix} \begin{bmatrix} 2 & 1 \\ 3 & 4 \end{bmatrix}$

$\mathbf{A}(\mathbf{BC}) = \begin{bmatrix} 4 & 2 & 8 \\ 3 & 3 & 7 \end{bmatrix} \begin{bmatrix} 14 & 17 \\ 15 & 10 \\ 37 & 41 \end{bmatrix}$

Both products are $\begin{bmatrix} 382 & 416 \\ 346 & 368 \end{bmatrix}$

Numbers and matrices both follow the **associative** rule for multiplication. However, although numbers follow the **commutative** law of multiplication you saw in question 1 that this law does not hold for matrices. Also, while any two numbers may be multiplied the same is not true of matrices. The matrix product **AB** can be formed only if the number of rows in **B** is equal to the number of columns in **A**; the two matrices are then said to be **compatible** for multiplication. You will see that **BA** and **C** are not compatible for multiplication and so the product (**BA**)**C** cannot be found.

3. (a) $\begin{bmatrix} 14 & 0 \\ 0 & 14 \end{bmatrix}$ (b) $\begin{bmatrix} 9 \\ 20 \end{bmatrix}$ (c) $\begin{bmatrix} 0.30 \\ 0.55 \\ 0.15 \end{bmatrix}$

4. (a) $\mathbf{T}^2 = \begin{bmatrix} \frac{3}{4} & \frac{1}{2} \\ \frac{1}{4} & \frac{1}{2} \end{bmatrix} \begin{bmatrix} \frac{3}{4} & \frac{1}{2} \\ \frac{1}{4} & \frac{1}{2} \end{bmatrix} = \begin{bmatrix} \frac{11}{16} & \frac{5}{8} \\ \frac{5}{16} & \frac{3}{8} \end{bmatrix}$

(b) $\mathbf{TV}_2 = \begin{bmatrix} \frac{3}{4} & \frac{1}{2} \\ \frac{1}{4} & \frac{1}{2} \end{bmatrix} \begin{bmatrix} \frac{3}{4} \\ \frac{1}{4} \end{bmatrix} = \begin{bmatrix} \frac{11}{16} \\ \frac{5}{16} \end{bmatrix}$

(continued)

(c) $\quad T^2V_1 = \begin{bmatrix} \frac{11}{16} & \frac{5}{8} \\ \frac{5}{16} & \frac{3}{8} \end{bmatrix} \begin{bmatrix} 1 \\ 0 \end{bmatrix} = \begin{bmatrix} \frac{11}{16} \\ \frac{5}{16} \end{bmatrix}$

$T^2V_1 = TV_2$. This is a consequence of the associative law:

$T^2V_1 = (TT)V_1 = T(TV_1) = TV_2.$

5.   **Either** follow the sequence V_1, $V_2 = TV_1$, $V_3 = TV_2$, ...

$$V_3 = TV_2 = \begin{bmatrix} \frac{11}{16} \\ \frac{5}{16} \end{bmatrix}, \quad V_4 = TV_3 = \begin{bmatrix} \frac{43}{64} \\ \frac{21}{64} \end{bmatrix}$$

$$V_5 = TV_4 = \begin{bmatrix} \frac{171}{256} \\ \frac{85}{256} \end{bmatrix} \approx \begin{bmatrix} 0.67 \\ 0.33 \end{bmatrix}$$

or express V_5 as T^4V_1:

$$T^4 = (T^2)^2 = \begin{bmatrix} \frac{11}{16} & \frac{5}{8} \\ \frac{5}{16} & \frac{3}{8} \end{bmatrix} \begin{bmatrix} \frac{11}{16} & \frac{5}{8} \\ \frac{5}{16} & \frac{3}{8} \end{bmatrix} \approx \begin{bmatrix} 0.67 & 0.66 \\ 0.33 & 0.34 \end{bmatrix}$$

$$V_5 = T^4 V_1 \approx \begin{bmatrix} 0.67 & 0.66 \\ 0.33 & 0.34 \end{bmatrix} \begin{bmatrix} 1 \\ 0 \end{bmatrix} = \begin{bmatrix} 0.67 \\ 0.33 \end{bmatrix}$$

1.

	C	S
C	20	30
S	29	20

2. $T = \begin{bmatrix} 0.41 & 0.60 \\ 0.59 & 0.40 \end{bmatrix} \approx \begin{bmatrix} 0.4 & 0.6 \\ 0.6 & 0.4 \end{bmatrix}$

3. $T^2 = \begin{bmatrix} 0.522 & 0.485 \\ 0.478 & 0.515 \end{bmatrix}$ or $\begin{bmatrix} 0.52 & 0.48 \\ 0.48 & 0.52 \end{bmatrix}$

4. If V is the outcome vector for any goal then the outcome probability vector for the next is TV and the vector for the goal after that is $T(TV) = T^2V$.

5. Frequency table:

		Last goal but one	
		C	S
This goal	C	29	21
	S	19	29

Transition matrix of probabilities: $\begin{bmatrix} 0.60 & 0.42 \\ 0.40 & 0.58 \end{bmatrix}$

6. The match between this matrix and T^2 is not close enough to accept the Markov chain model for Ashbourne ball game results.

Eigenvectors

SEQUENCES OF RANDOM EVENTS

COMMENTARY

TASKSHEET 3E

1. (a) $\mathbf{V}_1 = \begin{bmatrix} 0.4 \\ 0.6 \end{bmatrix}$, $\mathbf{V}_2 = \begin{bmatrix} 0.52 \\ 0.48 \end{bmatrix}$

    (b) $\begin{bmatrix} 0.7 & 0.4 \\ 0.3 & 0.6 \end{bmatrix} \begin{bmatrix} 4/7 \\ 3/7 \end{bmatrix} = \begin{bmatrix} 4/7 \\ 3/7 \end{bmatrix}$

2. All the points lie on the line $x + y = 1$.

3. The sequence $\mathbf{V}_0$, $\mathbf{V}_1$, $\mathbf{V}_2$, ... appears to be tending to the point $\mathbf{V}$. Again, all the points lie on the line $x + y = 1$.

    In fact, the distances to $\mathbf{V}$ of successive members of the sequence are in the ratio of $10 : 3$.

    This can be proved as follows:

    $$\begin{bmatrix} 0.7 & 0.4 \\ 0.3 & 0.6 \end{bmatrix} \begin{bmatrix} 4/7 + \epsilon \\ 3/7 - \epsilon \end{bmatrix} = \begin{bmatrix} 4/7 + 0.3\epsilon \\ 3/7 - 0.3\epsilon \end{bmatrix}$$

4. (a) For $\begin{bmatrix} x \\ y \end{bmatrix}$ on l, $x + y = 1$

    $$\begin{bmatrix} x' \\ y' \end{bmatrix} = \begin{bmatrix} 0.7 & 0.4 \\ 0.3 & 0.6 \end{bmatrix} \begin{bmatrix} x \\ 1-x \end{bmatrix} = \begin{bmatrix} 0.4 + 0.3x \\ 0.6 - 0.3x \end{bmatrix}$$

    Then $x' + y' = 1$ and so $\begin{bmatrix} x' \\ y' \end{bmatrix}$ is on l.

    (b) The result is true for any stochastic matrix $\begin{bmatrix} a & b \\ c & d \end{bmatrix}$. For such a matrix, $a + c = b + d = 1$.

    $$\begin{bmatrix} x' \\ y' \end{bmatrix} = \begin{bmatrix} a & b \\ c & d \end{bmatrix} \begin{bmatrix} x \\ 1-x \end{bmatrix} = \begin{bmatrix} b + (a-b)x \\ d + (c-d)x \end{bmatrix}$$

    Then $x' + y' = b + d + [(a + c) - (b + d)] x$
    $$= 1$$

    The significance of this is that if $\mathbf{v}$ is any outcome probability vector then $\mathbf{Tv}$ is also such a vector.

(continued)

5.   (a) $\begin{bmatrix} 0.7 & 0.4 \\ 0.3 & 0.6 \end{bmatrix} \begin{bmatrix} 1 \\ -1 \end{bmatrix} = \begin{bmatrix} 0.3 \\ -0.3 \end{bmatrix} = 0.3 \begin{bmatrix} 1 \\ -1 \end{bmatrix}$

       (b)   For the stochastic matrix $\begin{bmatrix} a & b \\ c & d \end{bmatrix}$,

$$a + c = b + d \implies a - b = -(c - d). \quad (\text{probabilities})$$

          Then $\begin{bmatrix} a & b \\ c & d \end{bmatrix} \begin{bmatrix} 1 \\ -1 \end{bmatrix} = \begin{bmatrix} a-b \\ c-d \end{bmatrix} = (a - b) \begin{bmatrix} 1 \\ -1 \end{bmatrix}$

6.   (a)   Any multiple of the steady state vector, $\frac{1}{7} \begin{bmatrix} 4 \\ 3 \end{bmatrix}$, is an eigenvector with eigenvalue 1.   ✓

       (b) $\mathbf{Tv} = \mathbf{T}\left(a \begin{bmatrix} 4 \\ 3 \end{bmatrix} + b \begin{bmatrix} 1 \\ -1 \end{bmatrix} \right)$

$$= a\mathbf{T} \begin{bmatrix} 4 \\ 3 \end{bmatrix} + b\mathbf{T} \begin{bmatrix} 1 \\ -1 \end{bmatrix}$$

$$= a \begin{bmatrix} 4 \\ 3 \end{bmatrix} + 0.3b \begin{bmatrix} 1 \\ -1 \end{bmatrix}$$

$$\mathbf{T}^n \mathbf{v} = a \begin{bmatrix} 4 \\ 3 \end{bmatrix} + 0.3^n b \begin{bmatrix} 1 \\ -1 \end{bmatrix}$$

       (c) $a = \frac{1}{7}$.

$$\mathbf{T}^n \mathbf{v} = \frac{1}{7} \begin{bmatrix} 4 \\ 3 \end{bmatrix} + 0.3^n b \begin{bmatrix} 1 \\ -1 \end{bmatrix} \rightarrow \frac{1}{7} \begin{bmatrix} 4 \\ 3 \end{bmatrix}$$

7.   (a)   For any point (x, y, z) on the plane $x + y + z = 1$,

$$\mathbf{T} \begin{bmatrix} x \\ y \\ z \end{bmatrix} \text{ also lies on the plane.}$$

       (b) $\begin{bmatrix} x' \\ y' \\ z' \end{bmatrix} = \begin{bmatrix} 0.3 & 0.1 & 0.4 \\ 0.3 & 0.2 & 0.2 \\ 0.4 & 0.7 & 0.4 \end{bmatrix} \begin{bmatrix} x \\ y \\ 1-x-y \end{bmatrix} = \begin{bmatrix} 0.4 - 0.1x - 0.3y \\ 0.2 + 0.1x \\ 0.4 \quad\quad + 0.3y \end{bmatrix}$

          Then $x' + y' + z' = 1$, as required.

1.　(a)　$\begin{bmatrix} \frac{1}{3} \\ \frac{2}{3} \end{bmatrix}$

　　(b)　If the steady state vector is $\begin{bmatrix} p \\ q \\ r \end{bmatrix}$ then

$$\frac{1}{2}p \qquad +\frac{1}{3}r = p$$

$$\frac{1}{2}p + \frac{1}{2}q +\frac{1}{3}r = q$$

$$\frac{1}{2}q +\frac{1}{3}r = r$$

From these equations, $p : q : r = 2 : 4 : 3$

$$p = \frac{2}{9}, \; q = \frac{4}{9}, \; r = \frac{1}{3}.$$

2.　The transition matrix is

$$\mathbf{T} = \begin{array}{c} P \\ S \end{array} \begin{matrix} \;\;\; P \;\;\;\;\; S \\ \begin{bmatrix} 0.2 & 0.4 \\ 0.8 & 0.6 \end{bmatrix} \end{matrix}$$

　　(a)　The outcome probability vector for the third day is $\mathbf{T}^2\mathbf{V}_1$,

where $\mathbf{V}_1 = \begin{bmatrix} 1 \\ 0 \end{bmatrix}$.

Then $\mathbf{TV}_1 = \begin{bmatrix} 0.2 \\ 0.8 \end{bmatrix}$ and $\mathbf{T}^2\mathbf{V}_1 = \begin{bmatrix} 0.36 \\ 0.64 \end{bmatrix}$

The probabilities of packed lunch and school meal are 0.36 and 0.64 respectively.

　　(b)　The appropriate vector $\mathbf{V}$ is the steady state vector given by $\mathbf{TV} = \mathbf{V}$.

If $\mathbf{V} = \begin{bmatrix} p \\ q \end{bmatrix}$ then $q = 1 - p$ and

$$0.2p + 0.4q = p$$
$$0.8p + 0.6q = q.$$

Then $p : q = 1 : 2$.

On the last day of term the corresponding probabilities are $\frac{1}{3}$ and $\frac{2}{3}$, respectively.

(continued)

38

3. (a)

$$\begin{bmatrix} \frac{1}{2} & \frac{1}{2} & 0 \\ 0 & \frac{1}{3} & \frac{2}{3} \\ \frac{1}{2} & \frac{1}{6} & \frac{1}{3} \end{bmatrix} \begin{bmatrix} \frac{1}{3} \\ \frac{1}{3} \\ \frac{1}{3} \end{bmatrix} = \begin{bmatrix} \frac{1}{3} \\ \frac{1}{3} \\ \frac{1}{3} \end{bmatrix}$$

(b) If $\begin{bmatrix} a \, b \, c \end{bmatrix}$ is any row of the matrix $\mathbf{T}$, then $a + b + c = 1$.

So $\begin{bmatrix} a \, b \, c \end{bmatrix} \begin{bmatrix} \frac{1}{3} \\ \frac{1}{3} \\ \frac{1}{3} \end{bmatrix} = \begin{bmatrix} \frac{1}{3}a + \frac{1}{3}b + \frac{1}{3}c \end{bmatrix} = \begin{bmatrix} \frac{1}{3} \end{bmatrix}$

Then $\mathbf{T} \begin{bmatrix} \frac{1}{3} \\ \frac{1}{3} \\ \frac{1}{3} \end{bmatrix} = \begin{bmatrix} \frac{1}{3} \\ \frac{1}{3} \\ \frac{1}{3} \end{bmatrix}$, as required.

39

5 *Simulation*

5.1   Introduction

> Three fair coins are tossed. After each toss those coins that come up heads are removed and the remaining coins are tossed again. This is repeated until no coins are left.
>
> (a)   Perform this experiment a number of times to obtain an estimate of the average number of tosses needed to remove all the coins.
>
> (b)   Use a computer or programmable calculator to simulate the experiment a large number of times. Hence obtain an improved estimate of the average number of tosses.
>
> (c)   Use the probability theory you have learnt in this unit to analyse the procedure.

(a)   A typical set of 10 results for this experiment might be

8, 2, 3, 2, 3, 4, 3, 1, 4, 6.

The average number of tosses needed in this case is 3.6. However, the data are so variable that you would have little confidence in this result.

(b)   A simple program, such as the following BBC BASIC program, will simulate the tossing of the coins.

```
10   C = 3: N = 0                              C is the number of coins.

20   X = 0                             ⎫  C is replaced by the
30   FOR I = 1 TO C : X = X + RND(2) – 1 : NEXT I  ⎬  number remaining after
40   C = X                             ⎭  tossing the coins.

50   N = N + 1                                 N is the number of tosses.
60   IF C > 0 THEN GO TO 20                     The coins are tossed until
70   PRINT N                                    C is zero.
```

The program can easily be modified to count the total number of tosses for a large number of experiments. Repeating the above program 10 000 times yielded 31 469 tosses i.e. an average of 3.1469 tosses per experiment.

Running such a simulation a number of times is likely to convince you that the average number of tosses is just greater than 3.

(c)   There are a number of ways in which you could try to analyse this situation.

Binomial probabilities

The probability that a particular coin still remains after n tosses is $\left(\frac{1}{2}\right)^n$. The probability that it does **not** remain after n tosses is therefore

$$\left[1-\left(\tfrac{1}{2}\right)^n\right].$$

The probability that **no** coin remains after n tosses is then $\left[1-\left(\tfrac{1}{2}\right)^n\right]^3$.

The probability that **precisely** n tosses are needed is therefore

$$p_n = \left[1-\left(\tfrac{1}{2}\right)^n\right]^3 - \left[1-\left(\tfrac{1}{2}\right)^{n-1}\right]^3.$$

Substituting values for n, the following results are obtained

n	p_n
1	$\left(\tfrac{1}{2}\right)^3 - 0^3 = 0.125$
2	$\left(\tfrac{3}{4}\right)^3 - \left(\tfrac{1}{2}\right)^3 \approx 0.297$
3	$\left(\tfrac{7}{8}\right)^3 - \left(\tfrac{3}{4}\right)^3 \approx 0.248$

and so on.

The mathematics so far has been tricky enough but the problem is still not solved. The average number of throws needed is given by $1 \times p_1 + 2 \times p_2 + 3 \times p_3 + \ldots$

$$\text{i.e. } \sum_{1}^{\infty} n\left(\left[1-\left(\tfrac{1}{2}\right)^n\right]^3 - \left[1-\left(\tfrac{1}{2}\right)^{n-1}\right]^3\right)$$

It is possible, but by no means easy, to sum this series. Whilst this is a worthwhile challenge for some students, others might prefer to look for a simpler method.

Renewal and recurrence relations

Consider the simpler problem of tossing a single coin until it comes up heads.

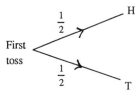

There is a probability $\frac{1}{2}$ that only one toss is needed and a probability $\frac{1}{2}$ that the situation **renews** itself.

If N_1 is the average number of tosses needed to remove one coin, then the renewal diagram gives

Number of tosses	probability
1	$\frac{1}{2}$
$1 + N_1$	$\frac{1}{2}$

Then $N_1 = \frac{1}{2} \times 1 + \frac{1}{2} \times (1 + N_1)$

$\Rightarrow N_1 = 1 + \frac{1}{2} N_1$

$\Rightarrow N_1 = 2$

A renewal diagram for two coins is

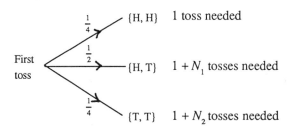

$\{H, H\}$ 1 toss needed

$\{H, T\}$ $1 + N_1$ tosses needed

$\{T, T\}$ $1 + N_2$ tosses needed

So $N_2 = \frac{1}{4} \times 1 + \frac{1}{2} \times (1 + N_1) + \frac{1}{4}(1 + N_2)$

$\Rightarrow N_2 = 1 + \frac{1}{2} N_1 + \frac{1}{4} N_2$

$\Rightarrow N_2 = \frac{8}{3}$

For three coins, the recurrence relation is

$$N_3 = 1 + \frac{3}{8} N_1 + \frac{3}{8} N_2 + \frac{1}{8} N_3$$

$$\Rightarrow N_3 = \frac{22}{7} \approx 3.143$$

Using considerable ingenuity, an analytical solution of the coin tossing problem has been obtained. However, the mathematics, even for this apparently simple problem, has been sufficiently complicated to demonstrate how useful simulations are likely to be when situations become much more involved.

Profiting from simulation

1. The expenditure and income for the project could be simulated using the following arrangement.

Expenditure £	Random Numbers
60 000	00-29
40 000	30-59
30 000	60-89
20 000	90-99

Income £	Random Numbers
120 000	00-09
80 000	10-49
60 000	50-89
20 000	90-99

The simulated profit would be obtained by randomly selecting (2-figure random numbers) income and expenditure. The experiment should be repeated a large number of times.

2.

Random Number	Expenditure £	Random Number	Income £	Profit
68	30 000	04	120 000	90 000
51	40 000	79	60 000	20 000
47	40 000	44	80 000	40 000
49	40 000	98	20 000	−20 000 (Loss)
90	20 000	21	80 000	60 000
71	30 000	52	60 000	30 000
41	40 000	64	60 000	20 000
68	30 000	04	120 000	90 000
23	60 000	76	60 000	0
10	60 000	09	120 000	60 000

3. The graphs for actual expenditure and income from 100 trials might be as shown below.

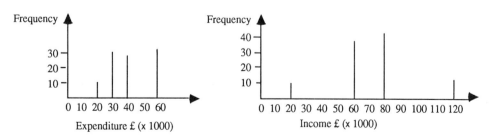

Your graphs should approximate to the empirical probability distributions.

(continued)

4. The graph below shows a risk profile from one hundred trials. Yours should be similar.

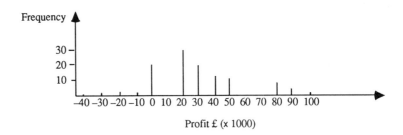

Profit £ (x 1000)

5. The simulation indicates that a loss is unlikely. On average, a substantial profit can be expected. Funds should be allocated to this project.

6. On average, the expenditure is

$£0.3 \times 60\,000 + 0.3 \times 40\,000 + 0.3 \times 30\,000 + 0.1 \times 20\,000$

$= £41\,000$

and the income is

$£0.1 \times 12\,0000 + 0.4 \times 80\,000 + 0.4 \times 60\,000 + 0.1 \times 20\,000$

$= £59\,200$ $= £70000$

The average profit is £18 200.   £29000

For this simple problem a simulation was **not** necessary. However, in more realistic and complex situations simulation is often the only feasible way to tackle the problem.

Tutorial sheet

1. The following BBC BASIC program generates the lengths of successive runs:

    ```
    10  F = RND(2)
    20  N = 1
    30  X = RND(2)
    40  IF X = F THEN N = N + 1 : GOTO 30
    50  PRINT N
    60  F = X : GOTO 20
    ```

    } The first 'toss' starts a run.

    } N counts the length of a run.

    A new run is started.

    A frequency table can then be drawn up by hand or the program can be modified to print out an appropriate table. The first 1600 runs for one computer simulation were as follows:

Run length	1	2	3	4	5	6	7	8	9	10	11	12
Frequency	794	409	197	95	42	31	14	9	4	3	0	2

    The frequencies roughly follow the pattern 800, 400, 200, 100, 50, 25, ... This should have been expected because:

    a run of length 1, XX' , has probability $1 \times \frac{1}{2} = \frac{1}{2}$,

    a run of length 2, XXX' , has probability $1 \times \frac{1}{2} \times \frac{1}{2} = \frac{1}{4}$,

    etc.

2. A routine such as the following can be used to simulate the lifetime of one battery:

    ```
    10  LET X = 500*RND(1) : Y = 0.01*RND(1)
    20  IF Y > 0.01*EXP(– 0.01*X) THEN GOTO 10
    30  PRINT X
    ```

    This could be incorporated in a program to find the lifetime of a torch. Alternatively, you could use a sequence of battery lifetimes to draw up a table as below and then make further calculations by hand.

Battery 1	Battery 2	Battery 3	Replacement time (hours)
34	112	161	34
...	...	...	...

    The average time before a battery needs replacing can be proved to be $\frac{100}{3}$ hours. You should obtain a time roughly equal to this.

45